Original title:
Feathers in the Dark

Copyright © 2025 Creative Arts Management OÜ
All rights reserved.

Author: Christian Leclair
ISBN HARDBACK: 978-1-80586-175-1
ISBN PAPERBACK: 978-1-80586-647-3

Enchanted Silhouettes

In shadows where giggles dare to play,
Dancing shadows twirl and sway.
A mouse in a hat, a cat in a shoe,
Hiding behind, it giggles too!

Goblins make tea with a sprinkle of cheese,
While owls play cards, laughing with ease.
The moon cracks jokes as the stars hold their sides,
In a ruckus of spirits where laughter abides.

In the Company of Night

Laughter erupts in the midnight hour,
As owls wear glasses and take a shower.
A raccoon spins tales of daring afar,
While foxes hold banquets with treats from the jar.

The glowworms flash like a disco ball,
With beetles that waltz, having a ball.
Crickets compose tunes on invisible strings,
Creating a symphony fit for all kings.

Glow of Celestial Echoes

A comet sneezes with a sparkling flare,
As constellations giggle without a care.
Planets mock Venus for being so bright,
In the cosmic café, everyone's polite.

Shooting stars play tag, dodging the moon,
Each stitch of light hums a humorous tune.
Galactic jesters juggle comets with glee,
In a universe bursting with wild jubilee.

The Color of Shadowed Flights

Bats in tuxedos take to the skies,
With ties that shimmer, they synchronise.
A crow makes a quip about fashion so bold,
As squirrels spin tales the night has told.

Whispers of laughter flit from tree to tree,
As crickets form choirs, joined in esprit.
With antics galore, the nocturnal parade,
Spins funny tales that shall never fade.

Luminous Shadows

In a realm where echoes play,
A light that's never gray.
The shadows dance, so spry,
With giggles that make time fly.

Tiny creatures with a flair,
Flap through the midnight air.
They trip on dreams like tramps,
In twilight's silly camps.

Velvet Whispers

Softly gliding through the night,
With mischief that feels just right.
Pillow fights with moonbeams bright,
And laughter fills the flight.

Hushed secrets shared with glee,
In the dark, so carefree.
Tickled by a breeze so sly,
As giggles soar up high.

The Dance of Ghostly Wings

In the mist, they swirl around,
With twirls that make no sound.
Invisible, they sway and glide,
Chasing giggles that won't hide.

A raucous party for the brave,
In shadows where laughs behave.
Wings flapping, what a sight,
A comedy in the night!

Beneath the Moon's Embrace

Beneath the glow, a prankish scene,
With shadows that laugh, pretty keen.
Tickling toes and swirling crowns,
The night wears silly gowns.

Forgotten spells in a wink,
Making the quite clean blink.
In cosmic giggles we'll embark,
Joy awaits within the dark.

Nighttime Serenade

Whispers of giggles float through the air,
A dance of shadows without a care.
Kittens on rooftops having their fun,
Under the moonlight, they prance and run.

Uncle Owl hoots a tune so sweet,
While mice toe-tap with tiny feet.
Bats wearing sunglasses swoop on by,
This nightly ruckus makes stars sigh.

Wings Against the Silent Breeze

Bubbles of laughter pop in the sky,
As clumsy birds trip and flail, oh my!
They think they're graceful, but we all know,
They're quite the comical nighttime show.

A squirrel joins in with a nut in tow,
While shadows gather for a lively throw.
A dance-off erupts, all feathers in flight,
Under the glow of the twinkling night.

The Soft Hug of Night

The night wraps all in a blanket of fun,
With mischief and madness till rising sun.
A raccoon juggles snacks with flair,
While crickets cheer from their leafy chair.

The stars giggle like kids in a game,
As clouds laugh along, calling out names.
The moon winks down like a friendly chap,
Inviting all to this whimsical flap.

Enchanted Flightpaths

A fizzy drink made of moonbeam juice,
Sips of delight from the night's filed clues.
The owls exchange jokes, quite a hoot,
While the fireflies shine, disco ball loot.

Each whimsy winged wanderer plays,
Floating through laughs in nocturnal arrays.
Their tales twist and turn in mid-air ballet,
In this whimsical world where we all want to stay.

The Allure of Obsidian Wings

In night's embrace, they flit and twirl,
Clumsy dancers in a hidden whirl.
With goofy grace, they glide and sway,
Leaving giggles in their feathery play.

They've lost their way in the moonlight glow,
Chasing shadows, oh where did they go?
With every flap, a comical fright,
Turning our dreams into laughter-filled night.

The Mystery of the Veiled Celestial

Oh, what secrets hide in darkened skies?
An almost laugh with curious sighs.
Who knew the stars wore such funny hats?
A party up there with celestial spats!

They wink and blink, such mischief they weave,
As planets play pranks, one can hardly believe.
Asteroids tumbling with a slapstick flair,
Making space silly, as they float without care.

Shadowed Grace of the Universe

In shadows soft, they dip and dive,
Wobbling through dreams, they come alive.
With cheeky spins and awkward plots,
Creating chuckles, connecting dots.

Mysterious forms that bob and weave,
Stealing laughter, what do they achieve?
A universe painted in giggling hues,
Where even the stars can't help but amuse.

Echoing Lullabies of the Night

In the stillness, they hum a tune,
A silly serenade by the silvery moon.
With each quirky note that fills the air,
It's a nighttime giggle, beyond compare.

Under soft blankets, the whispers creep,
As giggling shadows coax us to sleep.
Yet every lullaby has a twist,
Turning dreams into joy, you can't resist!

A Symphony of the Unseen

In twilight's grasp, a hiccup sings,
The moonlight dances, doing flings.
With giggles lost in shadow play,
Invisible notes make night a ballet.

Stars wink cheekily from their thrones,
While crickets beat on tiny bones.
A symphony we hear, yet can't see,
As shadows shimmy with glee.

Dreams of Celestial Wings

In a realm where laughter flies,
Giggling stars wear velvet ties.
Bouncing on the clouds like prods,
Chasing dreams in merry squads.

Plump little moons with jolly grins,
Join our frolic, let fun begin!
Whispers of starlight tease the air,
As giggly breezes comb our hair.

The Murmur of Velvet Shadows

Oh, the whispers of the night!
Shadows chuckle, what a sight!
Pillow fights with unseen foes,
Laughter hides as the darkness grows.

Fluffy forms in muted hues,
Tickle fights with silly snooze.
A shadowy waltz that makes you grin,
As stars spin laughter, let's join in!

Illusions of the Skybound

High above in laughter's lair,
Jokes are brewing in the air.
Clouds hide antics, whispers bright,
And stars dare each other to take flight.

The sky is cracked with cosmic cheer,
Echoes of giggles we can hear.
Chasing dreams on wobbly beams,
We laugh aloud, or so it seems.

Enchanted Shadows Take Flight

In the night, a giggle floats,
Chasing shadows, playful goats.
Some wear hats, a sight to see,
Dancing whims, wild and free.

Laughter rides on wings of dreams,
Wobbly ducks join in the schemes.
Through the stars they twirl and glide,
In the dark, their joy can't hide.

The Calm Before the Feathered Storm

A whisper stirs, the air is thick,
Silly birds prepare their tricks.
Pillow fights with clouds at dawn,
Who knew chaos could be so fun?

Fluffy tails and silly squawks,
Jokes exchanged with beak and talks.
Gather 'round, the antics start,
As laughter dances heart to heart.

Hushed Elegance of the Unknown

In the midnight, who's that there?
A wiggly worm with fancy flair.
Dressed in sparkles, what a sight,
Slinking softly, oh, what a flight!

Moonlit giggles echo near,
As shadows hide, yet persevere.
With grace they'll hop and prance anew,
A midnight ball, for me and you.

A Tapestry of Twilight Tails

Threads of laughter weave the night,
Tails that twirl, oh what a sight.
A squirrel with a monocle, so neat,
Dancing slowly, tapping feet.

Cats in capes quoting fine prose,
Juggling jiggly jelly by their toes.
In this fable, joy takes reign,
With silly games, there's nothing plain.

Shimmering Shadows

In a corner, a shadow does wink,
With twinkling eyes, it starts to think.
It whispers jokes to the chair and lamp,
Together they laugh, a giggling camp.

I stumble in, but they hush and freeze,
Pretending there's nothing to tease or please.
The chair just shrugs with a wooden grin,
And I can't help but join the din.

Laughter bounces off every wall,
I can't resist, I trip and fall.
The shadow chuckles, what a delight,
In this silly dance of shadowy light.

Lurking Beneath the Feathered Veil

Under a blanket of dust and gloom,
A creature cackles in its cozy room.
With a quill and ink, it scribbles a tale,
Of socks that vanished, of dreams gone stale.

It plots and plans, this sneaky sprite,
In a game of hide and seek at midnight.
With each twist of the pen, it twists my fate,
For it knows that laughter can never wait.

"Here's the punchline!" it cries with glee,
As the socks laugh back, "Just let us be!"
Oh, the antics of socks and sprites at play,
In the depths of night, they dance and sway.

Concealed in Veils of Night

A creature dons a cloak of fright,
It hides away in the dead of night.
With a silly hat atop its head,
It dreams of donuts and soft, warm bread.

Its antics echo with muffled cheer,
As it throws pillows, there's nothing to fear.
"I'm just a ghost!" it giggles with glee,
"Can't haunt you right if you can't see me!"

Lurking low, it sings a tune,
To lure in the stars and the glowing moon.
They chuckle aloud at its playful guise,
As it dances 'round in its feathered lies.

Harbingers of Silence

In a quiet room where whispers creep,
Lies a band of misfits not prone to sleep.
They plot and they plan in gleeful hush,
To break the silence with a ridiculous rush.

"Shh!" says one with a snicker and grin,
"Let's blow the night sky and let chaos in!"
With marshmallow bombs and laughter loud,
Their mischief turns solemn into a cloud.

In the midst of stillness, they cause a ruckus,
With jokes and giggles, they bring the circus.
So when you hear the stillness break,
Know it's just friends who love a good shake.

Silhouettes Beneath the Moonlit Sky

In the night, we prance and glide,
Chasing dreams we can't abide.
With shadows long, we tease the breeze,
And trip on laughs, like clumsy bees.

Giggles echo off the trees,
As we dance with silly ease.
A gang of ghouls, so full of cheer,
In the dark, we disappear.

Murmurs of the Twilight Breeze

The whispers play, the shadows hum,
As we tumble, oh so numb.
With a squeak and squeal, we march in line,
Who needs the sun? We're doing fine!

Giant moths, they bump and crash,
While we fumble in a flash.
In this dim-lit circus, we reunite,
Finding joy in playful fright.

A Dance of Shadows and Softness

Underneath the stars, we wiggle and twirl,
In the cloak of night, we spin and swirl.
A parade of giggles on a wobbly path,
Like marionettes caught in a laugh.

With all the grace of a floppy sock,
We juggle jokes and laugh at the clock.
As starlight tickles our funny bones,
We gather the night as if it's our own.

Hidden Colors in the Gloom

In the twilight, colors fade,
We bring the fun, unafraid.
With each stumble and silly stunt,
We paint the night, a vibrant hunt.

From shadows deep, the giggles rise,
As we create our own surprise.
In the eerie hush, we take our stand,
As goofy ghosts, we're a merry band.

Whispers of the Night

In the hush, a giggle sighs,
A chicken's joke makes owls cry.
Bats wear capes, they're quite the sight,
As crickets trade their puns at night.

The moon rolls her eyes, she's seen it all,
As mice perform their mini ball.
A flurry of feathers, a wild dance,
As fireflies blink—oh what a chance!

Squirrels gossip, nimble and spry,
With acorns flying, oh my, oh my!
Raccoons steal snacks with cheeky grace,
While shadows waltz in a merry race.

Secrets on Silent Wings

Who knew that owls had such flair?
They hold debates up in the air.
A whispered joke, a stolen glance,
Turned night into a wild dance.

Invisible secrets, laughter just near,
Imagine a fox in a sparkling tiere!
Hooting and tooting, the secrets expand,
As raccoons lead with a live band.

Mice in top hats, dancing with style,
Who knew night critters could be this vile?
A parade of shadows, with quirks and glee,
Just wait till you hear the late-night spree!

Shadows Cloaked in Plumage

Shadows pirouette, a curious crew,
Dressed in plumage of every hue.
Jokes on the wind, they flutter and swoop,
As laughter ripples through the troop.

A crow in a tux, with swagger to boot,
Tells tales of mischief, oh what a hoot!
The frogs croak punchlines, slick as can be,
As all join in nightly jubilee.

A dapper owl with a curious wink,
Sips moonlight tea, as stars start to blink.
Each feather a mask, nonsense takes flight,
In a cloak of confusion, the shadows ignite.

The Soft Embrace of Midnight

Midnight giggles, a soft little tease,
As slumbering creatures stir with ease.
Bats running late to their own soirée,
While stars pull pranks in a cosmic ballet.

A rabbit's laugh is quite the charade,
With floppy ears making the grand parade.
Cats roll their eyes, being oh so sly,
As the world above twinkles with a sigh.

The bushes rustle, secrets abound,
Mice tell tall tales, and giggles resound.
In the embrace of night, antics unfold,
With humorous whispers, the dark takes hold.

A Tapestry of Darkness

In shadows where giggles creep,
A cloak of night, secrets we keep.
With creatures that flutter and flap,
Cackling softly in a moonlit trap.

An owl in glasses reads the clock,
While squirrels dance in mismatched socks.
They argue about the best of snacks,
Under stars doing silly acts.

Winged Whispers of the Unknown

A crow once tried to tell a joke,
But all the pigeons just went 'yolk!'
They flapped their wings in sheer delight,
As bats joined in, what a sight!

Moths consider fashion so sleek,
In lampshade gowns, they truly peak.
The laughter echoes through the trees,
As moonlight sways with giggling breeze.

Whispers Beneath Starlit Veils

A raccoon sneaked with a shiny spoon,
While owls hooted in a funky tune.
The stars winked over the sly parade,
As shadows flickered, mischief made.

A fox wore spectacles just to boast,
While a porcupine shared ghost stories most.
The night played tricks, oh what a class,
With echoes of laughter that would not pass.

The Call of Hidden Wings

A parrot with a top hat sang,
While the night critters around him sprang.
The bats wore capes and flew a show,
And the chirps turned into a lively row.

A salamander played the flute,
As night turned silly and quite astute.
With hidden wings and twinkling eyes,
The fun took off beneath starry skies.

Beneath Twilight's Cloak

Under the veil where shadows play,
Silly things chase the night away.
A squirrel with a hat, quite the sight,
Dancing around, oh what a delight!

Giggles and whispers, a blend of cheer,
Jokes with owls, their wisdom clear.
Beneath the stars, we tiptoe along,
Bouncing to the beat of a night-time song.

Marshmallows float, light as a breeze,
While rabbits trade hats with mysterious ease.
The moon winks down as fireflies flit,
In this comical world, we never sit!

So gather your laughter, let spirits soar,
In twilight's embrace, we laugh even more.
For in this realm, where whimsy glows,
Every moment is gold, as everybody knows.

Shadows that Sing

In a garden where shadows hum,
Curly cues of giggles come.
Due to a frog that wears a crown,
Perched on a stone, he won't frown!

With shadows that dance in the cool night air,
It's hard not to chuckle, one must beware.
For a ghost with a grin roams near the tree,
Telling tall tales, most absurdly free.

A cat on a fence claims to speak French,
While squirrels debate how to climb a wrench.
And laughter erupts as the moonbeam plays,
Wrapping us all in a soft, silly haze.

So let your worries float far away,
Join in the fun, come out and play.
For shadows that sing under lovestruck skies,
Make even the dullest hearts rise and fly.

The Quiet Waltz of Elysian Wings

A dance of whimsy, soft as a sigh,
Where giggling sprites in the night do fly.
They duck and dive with cheeky glee,
Making the stars laugh, oh woe is he!

A moonlit soirée with frogs in a row,
Twirling in ruffles, putting on a show.
The fireflies flicker, they're part of the crew,
"Is it a ball? Or just a light brew?"

Dandy lions wear shoes, strut with pride,
While wise old crickets provide the guide.
Each twirl and swirl, a flurry of fun,
In a world where laughter weighs more than a ton.

Though silent the wings, the joy they share,
Is like tickles of sunshine in midnight air.
With every laugh echoes far and wide,
The quiet waltz becomes our guide.

Echoes of the Silvery Night

At dusk, where the quiet shadows leap,
A band of raccoons starts to creep.
In masks and tails, they play their pranks,
You'll laugh so hard, you'll have to give thanks!

The owls all hoot with the best of jokes,
While fireflies twinkle, like cheeky folks.
"Why did the nightingale sing so loud?"
"Because he saw a tumbleweed dancing proud!"

With echoes that shimmer in soft twilight,
Squirrels juggle acorns, oh what a sight!
In the giggly quiet, joy takes its stand,
As shadows stroll lightly, hand in hand.

So gather your friends, let merriment start,
With echoes that tickle the sweetest heart.
For in the silvery glow where laughter ignites,
The night becomes bright with such silly delights.

Insomniac Skylarks

A bird sat wide awake at two,
Counting stars and missing dew.
With a yawn, it fluffed its chest,
Said, 'I think I'll skip the rest.'

It chirped a song with a sleepy giggle,
To the moon, it did a little wiggle.
The owls just rolled their eyes with jest,
'When will you learn? Just take a rest!'

Meanwhile, squirrels were dancing near,
Confetti nuts tossed high in cheer.
Our skies were bright with their delight,
As daydreams turned to morning light.

By dawn's first blush, they sighed and played,
In every shade through branches swayed.
With dawn's embrace, they claimed their crown,
In the silly parade of sleepy towns.

The Song of Unseen Avian

In shadows, flutters, a secret tune,
Echoes beneath the laughing moon.
With beaks agape, they croaked and cawed,
Conducting chaos with wild applause.

A troupe of birds, oh what a sight,
Each with quirks and peculiar flight.
Through tangled trees and whispers lost,
They tumbled around, no matter the cost.

One claimed prowess of being wise,
But fumbled down from tree to skies.
The others chuckled, snickering loud,
A fool in feathers, veiled in pride's shroud.

They sang of grapes that grew on air,
Of sandwiches made without a care.
So here's to songs that we can't see,
In the twilight, where we laugh with glee.

Cloaked in Midnight's Embrace

In the quiet hours, cloaked in night,
The silly birds took off in flight.
They zoomed and zipped without a plan,
A feathered frenzy, a quirky clan.

With flappy wings, they spun in glee,
Brushing stars like it's some grand spree.
Nestled deep in a puffy cloud,
One lost their grip and yelled out loud!

'Hey, let's play tag around the moon!'
Shrieked the other, with a bright maroon.
But one got stuck in a comet's tail,
Coming down with a whoosh and a wail!

Yet they tumbled back to their nest,
With stories that had them far from stressed.
So here's to lights that tease and play,
In an evening dance that led them astray.

Enigmas on Silent Winds

A riddle crossed the evening breeze,
'What's fluffy, light, and loves to tease?'
The answer floated within a croak,
A comical twist of a feathered joke.

With parades of quirks, they wandered bold,
Chasing comets, both gleeful and cold.
They lost a hat while playing charades,
In a game of dashes and morning cascades.

A sly old crow rolled his eyes in jest,
Said, 'The punchline's lost; what a messy quest!'
While giggling thrushes flew in loops,
Debating the riddles like goofy troops.

Now somewhere in the whispering night,
Lost jokes drift in feathers alight.
With ups and downs, each jest replays,
As mysteries form in the starlit bays.

The Flight of Starlit Dreams

In the moon's glow, a chicken pranced,
Clucking secrets in a midnight dance,
Balloons were tied to every wing,
A silly sight, oh what a fling!

Stars winked down with a cheeky laugh,
As ducks in tutus took a bath,
They spread their wings, the night was ripe,
For laughter wrapped in feathered hype!

A crow played chess with a sleepy cat,
Who wore a mask, imagine that!
While owls played cards and sipped on tea,
Turning night into a comedy!

Then a parrot, full of glee,
Said, "Who needs sleep? Let's have a spree!"
And as the dawn burst forth in color,
They packed their dreams, thicker than a sailor!

Cloaked in the Silence of Night

In shadows deep, a squirrel snored,
Dreaming of acorns, slightly bored,
A hedgehog juggled under the stars,
Cracking jokes about credit bars!

Bats in bow ties flew by in glee,
As raccoons danced around a tree,
Their hats were tall, their style was chic,
Making mischief every week!

The fireflies blinked like disco lights,
As nighttime critters had silly fights,
A tortoise won a race—what a show!
While a snail claimed a gold medal, you know!

Then the moon winked, and the night chuckled,
With giggles from creatures mildly snuggled,
In this cloak of laughter, absurd and vast,
The darkness was poetry, unsurpassed!

Beneath the Velvet Horizon

Under a blanket of soft, dark blue,
The grasshoppers sang a funny tune,
With crickets tapping their tiny feet,
They formed a band, oh what a feat!

Fireflies drifted in a blinky blight,
Chasing their tails, oh what a sight!
A rabbit, quite proud, wore a hat on the run,
Said, "Hop along, it's all in good fun!"

Twirling turtles played hopscotch there,
While kittens rehearsed their stand-up flair,
A wise old owl perched high and bright,
Chiming in with thoughts of sheer delight!

As morning approached, they packed up tight,
With giggles echoing into the light,
Having painted the night with giggles and cheer,
Furry and feathered, they held it dear!

The Lullaby of Winged Nightfall

An owl hummed a tune that was quite absurd,
While squirrels played chess with a whimsical bird,
The moon laughed out loud as the stars joined in,
To serenade the night with whimsical spin!

A group of mice wore tiny pajamas,
And shared jokes about their grand mamas,
Telling tales of cheese heists in court,
With giggles and chuckles, their favorite sport!

Down below, rabbits did ballet in dew,
While turtles compared who had the best shoe,
Every creature had stories to share,
Dancing through dreams without a care!

So as the night wrapped the world in its cloak,
With twinkling tales and laughter evoked,
A melody lingered among the trees,
A lullaby of joy, carried on the breeze!

Invisible Pathways

In shadows where no light will tread,
A squirrel in a tux, so oddly spread.
He wobbles between the trees with glee,
Claiming all the nuts for his floppy tea.

A rabbit rolls a dice, what a sight!
He hops and skips and laughs with delight.
Yet loses to a turtle, slow and grand,
Chasing dreams in a race all unplanned.

The moon giggles with its twinkling grin,
As owls dance wildly, and the cats spin.
They throw confetti made of starlit dust,
In a midnight fiesta, just because they must.

So sip your juice from a tiny cup,
And join the fun as the sun comes up.
These paths are hidden, yet they guide,
To laughter's echoes where secrets abide.

Haunting Melodies in Twilight

A ghost with shades, oh what a sight,
He croons a tune in the fading light.
His voice a tickle, oh so absurd,
As bats take stage, their wings all blurred.

The shadows clap, they stomp and sway,
A skeleton band comes out to play.
With mismatched bones and a rusty drum,
They break into a jig, how can this be fun?

A cat in a top hat, playing the lute,
She strums a chord, and the vibes are cute.
Laughter echoes in the still of the night,
While owls take selfies, capturing delight.

What a concert, with giggles so bright,
As moonbeams twinkle, oh what a sight!
Hold your tummy, join their spree,
In this twilight gig, so wild and free.

A Dance in the Gloom

In gloom where shadows twirl and glide,
A bear on roller skates takes the ride.
He stomps and spins, a wobble parade,
A disco inferno, the dance floor's laid.

The fireflies flash in colors so gay,
While crickets chirp in their own ballet.
A frog leaps high, in a tutu so bright,
With dragonflies cheering, oh what a sight!

The moon plays DJ, spinning a tune,
As mice in tuxedos join the festoon.
They dance in circles, a waltz with a squawk,
Shaking their tails, in a midnight clock.

So hold on tight, and join their cue,
In this bizarre jive, where dreams come true.
For laughter lives in the twist and the whirl,
In the silly shadows where joys unfurl.

The Calm Between Feathers

In the still of night, a bird snores loud,
While a mouse in pajamas feels oh-so-proud.
They share a blanket made of twinkling stars,
And make toast with jam from the moonlit jars.

A hedgehog rolls in, with snacks galore,
He tells a tale of a dance on the floor.
In whispers soft, they giggle and jest,
About silly owls who just can't rest.

The quiet hums with mischief and glee,
As fireflies buzz, just wait and see!
A raccoon, mischievous, swipes a treat,
With cookies and milk, oh so sweet!

So cozy the night, with cuddly friends,
They share their dreams as the laughter blends.
In the calm of night, where silliness spreads,
In a haven of joy, where laughter threads.

Secrets of Midnight's Plumage

In shadows where giggles hide,
Pigeons dance with a silly stride.
They wear top hats, oh what a sight,
And moonbeams twirl in pure delight.

An owl tells jokes, a real hoot,
Wearing mismatched a feathered suit.
The stars chuckle, twinkle and tease,
As laughter floats on a playful breeze.

A bat appears with a funny flinch,
Claiming he's the prince, though he can't clinch.
The crickets laugh with a chirpy cheer,
As midnight paints its humor here.

In the night, all secrets unfold,
Where dreams wear shoes of silver and gold.
Sojoin the fun, don't be aloof,
Join the night's giggle, let it be proof.

Invisible Slumber

As night tiptoes with fluffy shoes,
The sandman's lost his map, oh, what a ruse!
Bunnies in pajamas hop with glee,
Whispering tales of what could be.

Dreams are painted like polka dots,
While snoring cats say, 'Stop the plots!'
A wink from the moon, a puff of sleep,
Silly secrets the night may keep.

Sleepyheads lounge with pizza slices,
Floating on clouds, oh, what nice vices!
They giggle as the dreaming unfolds,
In a comedy of dreams, so bold.

When dawn arrives with a funny grin,
They spill out laughter, let the day begin!
Ticklish sunbeams entice and pry,
As sleepy whispers bid night goodbye.

The Shadowed Sky's Embrace

In the embrace of the giggling night,
Stars wear pajamas, oh, what a sight!
Clouds play tag in the midnight air,
With shadows sneaking, unaware.

Mice in tuxedos dance with flair,
While owls critique every little stare.
The breeze tells jokes as it swirls around,
In this cheeky place, laughter is found.

A raccoon in shades strikes a pose,
Says, 'I'm the night's most stylish rose!'
The shadows giggle, a mischievous crew,
In a world where anything's funny and new.

As dawn peeks in with a hallelujah,
The night's secrets sprinkled like good ol' stew.
But hold your breath, don't let it part,
For laughter won't flee from the night's heart.

Untold Aspects of Twilight

When the clock strikes giggle, the fun begins,
The twilight's secrets wear silly grins.
Kittens in capes fly up to the trees,
Plotting their mischief with wobbly knees.

A squirrel dons glasses, seeks wisdom's way,
While fireflies wink, 'Come join our play!'
The stars burst forth like popcorn in air,
Tickled by night, without a care.

Twilight whispers, 'It's all a show!'
As shadows prance in a comical flow.
Each moment a dance, each dream a jest,
In the heart of the night, the laughter's a fest.

Embrace the silly, let the stories weave,
As twilight fades like a prank we believe.
For in this play, so wild and stark,
Lies the joy of living, in the vast and dark.

Cloaks of Downy Nightfall

Under stars, a sneaky cat,
Tiptoes softly, finding fat.
A shadow leaps, a startled quack,
In the night, ducks wear a hat.

A blanket thrown across the floor,
Socks are hiding, but there's more!
Giggles rise from every nook,
Nighttime's mischief, come take a look.

The moon's a jester, grinning wide,
While sleepy sheep begin to slide.
Wrapped in wool, they dream and bleat,
In cozy piles, their nightly seat.

Whispers echo, laughter blooms,
In the dark, a party zooms.
A dance of shadows, all in play,
As nighttime dreams drift far away.

Boundless Aether

A kite just flew away with glee,
Propelled by winds of whimsy spree.
It tugged a laugh from the tall trees,
As squirrels danced on branch and breeze.

The stars all wink, a cheeky crew,
They twinkle bright, like 'peek-a-boo.'
And in the moss, a toad takes flight,
With tiny wings, it claims the night.

The clouds play tag, a fluffy game,
While shadows stretch and shadows claim.
A giggling breeze, a joyful squeal,
Atop the hills, the world's surreal.

To dream in colors, bright and loud,
Awake the heart, unleash the proud.
With all this fun, oh, what a sight!
The sky's alive, a pure delight!

Shrouded in Silhouette

A stealthy frog upon the wall,
In shadows dark, it makes a call.
It croaks a tune, a funny song,
That echoes deep, where shadows throng.

A broomstick flies, a witch says, 'Whee!'
As owls and bats look on with glee.
Each twist and turn, a comical show,
In the moonlight's glow, they dance below.

A mouse in slippers, quite absurd,
Shoes too big, it rarely stirred.
But when it runs, oh what a sight,
It leaps and flails, a goofy rite.

These silhouettes in jest unite,
Underneath the moon's soft light.
The funny shapes that twist and twine,
In the night, they laugh, they shine.

Dusk's Watchful Eyes

With every blink, the world turns shy,
As shadows grow and softly sigh.
An unseen wink from owls on guard,
In the dimness, they work hard.

A lamp post wobbles, bats take flight,
With flappy antics, quite a sight.
The crickets chirp a silly beat,
As night unfolds its frolicking sheet.

A timid cat gives a loud purr,
It leaps and bounds like a furry blur.
In laughter shared, we find our way,
The night is ours, let's shout hooray!

So gather 'round, the fun's begun,
In dusk's embrace, we chase and run.
With whispers soft and giggles bright,
We dance together in the night.

A Dream Beyond the Wings of Dusk.

In twilight's glow, a chicken prances,
Claiming skies with fowl advances.
She flaps her wings, though she can't soar,
A dance of dreams on the kitchen floor.

Her friends all chuckle at her bold quest,
Clucking along, they find it the best.
A surfboard slide on a greasy plate,
Who knew dinner could be so great?

The moon beams down on this feathery crew,
While squirrels holler, 'Hey! What's new?'
They take a bow and then they flee,
Chasing shadows, in glee they agree.

With every flap and stumbling cheer,
Life's a circus here, never fear.
In the twilight's giggle, all bets are off,
Hopping and clucking, come join the scoff!

Whispers of the Night Sky

Up in the night, a bat complains,
While a parakeet snickers through the lanes.
"Why don't you dive?" croaked the chatty crow,
But the bat just grinned—'I'm not a pro!'

The stars twinkle, like tiny specks,
As a pigeon poses, flexing its pecs.
"Look at me!" it coos with pride,
While the owls roll eyes, trying to hide.

A rabbit hops with a jolly laugh,
"Dare you to fly? Let's split this half!"
With every chuckle, the night gets bright,
In this silly realm of pure delight.

The moon joins in, shedding silver light,
"Dance, my friends, let's take flight!"
And together they jive, under zephyr's sway,
Whispers of the night say, "Hip-hip-hooray!"

Shadows Take Flight

In the corner, a shadow sneezes,
With a whisper of giggles, it teases.
A playful breeze sends hats on a spin,
While cats proclaim, 'Let the games begin!'

An owl shimmies on a fence so proud,
Jiving with crickets, bouncing the crowd.
"Whooo's got the moves?" the raccoon shouts,
They giggle, never fearing doubts.

Bats flutter wildly in the fading light,
Joining the party, taking flight.
With every clap, the shadows do sway,
In this odd dance, they blend and play.

As laughter swirls like petals on air,
The world becomes a comedic affair.
So let your spirit lift and unite,
In this zany escapade, all fears take flight!

Silken Echoes at Twilight

In the dusk, a spider spins a tale,
Of feasts with jumpers, and tales to unveil.
While ladybugs cheer, itching to compete,
Dancing on webs, oh what a feat!

A frog croaks loudly, 'I can leap, just try!'
While a wise old tortoise watches nearby.
"Speed's overrated, my dear little friends,
Slow and steady, it's how the night bends."

With every hop and a curious glance,
The twinkling stars join in this grand dance.
Prancing about with shadows galore,
They giggle and glide on the twilight floor.

As laughter echoes through night's silken seam,
Creatures unite for a whimsical dream.
So join the soirée, don't miss the spark,
For shadows shine brightest, creating a mark!

Echoes of Dusk's Gentle Caress

In shadowed nooks, a giggle sneaks,
As whispers dance on twilight's cheeks.
A chorus springs from unseen wings,
With comedic chirps, the night clown sings.

Through tangled limbs, the pranksters flit,
With mischief laced in every wit.
A tumble here, a flutter there,
They zip around without a care.

Oh, how they tease, these playful sprites,
Darting through murky, starry nights.
A wink and nudge, a sly little jest,
In the soft hush, they never rest.

So in the dark, the laughter flows,
With punchlines tucked in sleepy prose.
Each moment bright with subtle fun,
'Til dawn's warm rays have gently spun.

Wings of Mystery Unfurled

In secret corners, giggling strong,
The whispers weave a comic song.
What's that shadow? A chuckle near,
As chaos blooms, from ear to ear.

A flock of quirks in stealthy flight,
With flappy jokes that take to night.
They flutter past a yawning moon,
And flip the script with comedic tune.

With every twist and every turn,
There's mischief that we crave to learn.
Twisted tales of nightly fun,
The giggling gang, they're on the run!

So when the dusk begins to call,
And laughter echoes through it all,
Hold tight your dreams, or they'll take wing,
In a playful jest, the dark will sing.

The Veil of Celestial Plumes

A veil of laughs, a cloak of glee,
Where night unfolds its mystery.
Silly shades with a darting gaze,
In twinkling flight, they start to raze.

With muted shrieks of feathered fun,
The night is filled, no more a shun.
Leaping forth from tangled shadows,
The time for jests and giggles grows.

Beneath the stars that wink and pop,
The capers rise, they'll never stop!
A tumble here, a playful twirl,
In midnight's grasp, they joyfully swirl.

In this realm, laughter finds its way,
With no regrets to chase away.
As moonlight guides their frolic spree,
A whimsical world, so wild and free.

Nocturnal Dreams of Sable Feathers

In dreams where echoes softly play,
The tricks of night lead us astray.
Shadows twist with laughter's zest,
A jokester's caper, their spunky fest.

With every flap, a jest unfolds,
In mysterious hues, a story told.
A chuckle here and wink over there,
It's a comedy show, without a care!

As starlight lends its playful gleam,
The giggling sprites weave through the dream.
Chasing laughs like teasing winds,
In fanciful spins, the mischief spins.

So let the night bring joyful cheer,
For laughter thrives in shadows near.
With every flutter of playful grace,
Night's laughter paints a smiling face.

Arcane Migrations

In shadows, the owls hoot and glance,
A dance of the pigeons in a playful prance.
The bats flip-flop, making quite a show,
As they juggle the stars in the moonlight glow.

Silly ghouls sway, trying to impress,
With glow-in-the-dark paint, it's quite a mess.
Crows crunch a snack of pizza from night,
Sipping on soda, feeling just right.

Mice on rollerblades speed down the lane,
In search of a party where cheese reigns.
Ducks quack in tune, holding a debate,
About who can waddle while looking first-rate.

So if you hear giggles beneath the night's veil,
Look closely for critters that won't fail.
They'll tickle your fancy, they'll steal the show,
In their whimsical world, just watch them go!

Dreaming in Dusk

In twilight's embrace, the squids wear hats,
Dancing with shadows, and chit-chat with cats.
Jellyfish float by tossing confetti,
While crabs put on skits, quite unsavory yet petty.

The owls wear glasses, reading the stars,
While raccoons debate over candy bars.
A parade of the odd, with a potato in tow,
Making a fuss with a loud 'whoa!' and 'whoa!'

Fireflies twinkle in mismatched socks,
As the turtles tune into their favorite knocks.
A raccoon DJ spins beats in the air,
While frogs hop around, dancing without a care.

So, when the sun dips and the laughter's near,
Join the fun—it's a magical sphere.
For in the hush, absurdity thrives,
With dreams that bounce as the night comes alive!

The Essence of Night's Embrace

Under a blanket of night's very best,
Squirrels debate which nut is the zest.
Cats play poker with their tails on display,
While goldfish gossip, sipping on whey.

The moon's a comedian, cracking wild jokes,
While foxes giggle and hop with the folks.
Owls throw a party—no need for a plan,
With a DJ raccoon who's the truest of fans.

As shadows grow long, the revelry peaks,
With lanterns made from learned mystic tweaks.
A parade of oddities slide down the street,
With penguins in tuxes presenting a feat.

So laugh in the night, let the whimsy sway,
In the essence of hide-and-seek, come what may.
Join in the giggles, escape to the dark,
Where the essence of fun leaves its bright mark!

A Veil of Winged Whispers

A cloud of chattering crickets at play,
In a symphony of nonsense, night turns to day.
When dragonflies dance with their wingtips so sly,
And moths in capes flutter on by.

A chorus of laughter echoes through trees,
As squirrels scamper, their frolic with ease.
Hooting owls banter about puns so absurd,
While frogs in tuxedos practice their words.

Under the starlight, the shadows all cheep,
As penguins slide down slopes, far from sleep.
Ghosts in the back hold a karaoke show,
While raccoons make ice cream, stealing the glow.

So bask in the laughter and humor they share,
With a veil of whispers that dance in the air.
The night's playful spirit cradles delight,
In a whimsical world of charm and of light!

Wings of Midnight

In twilight's embrace, the critters will laugh,
As shadows take flight, plotting mischief and craft.
With whispers of giggles, the night owl must sigh,
Those wings of mishap, oh my, oh my!

The raccoons hold court, all dressed up in style,
With masks on their faces, they pry for a while.
A chitter, a chatter, they dance on the ground,
In moonlight so bright, their silliness found.

Bats waltz through the trees, like dancers galore,
They twirl and they spin, in the cool nighttime lore.
A thud! Is it folly or someone's bad luck?
Oh, who's that? A possum just tripped over a truck!

Laughter rings out like a song in the night,
With critters at play, oh what a delight!
So when the sun sets, don't shy from the cheer,
For fun in the dark is always quite near.

Secrets Wrapped in Plumage

On velvety nights, a parrot does scheme,
With secrets to share that seem like a dream.
In the hush of the night, he whispers with flair,
That the best of the tales are found up in the air.

The sparrows convene for a chatterbox fest,
Trading tall tales with their fluffiest best.
A rumor on wind, it tickles the trees,
While owls just roll their eyes with such ease.

Pigeons in suits, they strut with such pride,
In their ties and their bows, they take every stride.
But when the moon giggles, they trip in a line,
And suddenly find their grand plans just unwind.

With every quirk and giggle, the night carries on,
Under starry canvases, silly stuff's drawn.
For secrets wrapped tight can unravel with glee,
As laughter ignites in this whimsical spree.

The Softest Shade of Dusk

When day bids goodbye with a wink and a grin,
A raccoon's parade of nonsense begins.
With a tip and a tap, they scamper around,
Their antics remind us of joys to be found.

The stars in the sky start to twinkle and tease,
As crickets create a night symphony, please!
A chorus of chirps, a melody sweet,
With imaginary hats, they stomp on their feet.

A hedgehog in socks, what a sight to behold,
Twirling with flair, he's brazen and bold.
With giggles and grins, the night melts away,
In the softest of shades, all troubles decay.

The moon casts her glow on the revelers' plight,
In this whimsical air, everything feels right.
So let's dance till dawn, in this silly parade,
Where fun and laughter shall never evade.

Night's Gentle Caress

In the hush of the night, a prankster delights,
With shadows at play, oh what silly sights!
Chirps turn to chuckles in the cool evening chill,
As critters embark on a comical thrill.

A marshmallow bunny hops by with a flip,
In over-sized shoes, he's ready to trip.
With laughter that echoes through silent trees,
Even owls crack a smile, swayed by the breeze.

The cat on the fence can't hide her disdain,
At the shenanigans causing her pain.
But underneath the moonshine, who can resist?
The allure of the night's merry, mad twist!

So let the stars shine on this wild, jovial spree,
For joy in the darkness is where we'll agree.
In night's gentle caress, we'll frolic and roam,
For the world is much brighter when laughter feels home.

Spirits of the Winged Night

In nighttime's cloak, the giggles rise,
Tiny flaps stir under starry skies.
Chasing shadows with a playful tease,
Teapot twirls in the gentle breeze.

Whispers bounce from tree to tree,
As owls wear hats for the jubilee.
Moonlight beams show the dance so bright,
It's a wings-on party deep in the night.

Splashing 'round puddles, oh what a sight,
Mischief unfolds with each flap in flight.
Laughter echoes through the twinkling spheres,
These spirits dance away all the fears.

With a swoosh and a swirl, they take to the air,
Tickling the stars, without a care.
As the night giggles, they glide and sway,
Join the fun, won't you, come out to play?

The Quiet Glide

Silent swooshes on a moonlit spree,
As shadows plot their prankery.
Beneath the canopy, giggling streams,
A secret party with silly dreams.

Masks of mystery and wings so wide,
They slip through trees on a feathered ride.
With every turn, laughter drips down,
Twinkling stars wear a giggling crown.

A whisper here, a snort on the breeze,
Dancing with limbs, they aim to please.
Daring stunts that cause a delight,
In the kingdom of shadows, all feels right.

Jumpy jests as they float and glide,
Creatures of whimsy, hearts full of pride.
By dawn's embrace, the mischief must cease,
But till then, we soar, finding our peace.

Murmurs of the Starlit Sky

Shapes swirl softly, with giggles and spins,
Moonlight giggles, as the fun begins.
Whispers dance like sparks in the air,
Backflips dashed between plump, fluffy hair.

Silly swoops, a ballet of jest,
Who knew the dark could hold such a fest?
With a wink and a flutter from tree to tree,
Joy spreads swiftly, wild and free.

Stars blink down at this lively parade,
A chorus of chuckles, well-played charade.
Every whoosh of wings is a quip in flight,
Fairy-tale antics under soft starlight.

Time jiggles funny, moments take wing,
In a realm where shadows do everything.
As dawn gently nudges this whimsy away,
The giggling echoes will long stay a-play.

Ethereal Drift of the Nocturne

Drifting through nights, with laughter so spry,
Chirpy chortles beneath the sky.
With a fluttering hush, they flip and float,
Roads of giggles where shadows gloat.

Dandelion dreams on a velvety sash,
Mixing moonbeams with some fancy hash.
Stars beyond flicker, join in the fun,
Playful frolics till the night is done.

Tempest of snickers, the echoes arise,
Twists of delight in the midnight ties.
With a sharp turn, they dash through the night,
Glued to the laughter that calls them to flight.

So gather around as the tales unfold,
Where laughter is silver and mischief is gold.
Each whimsy we share in this whimsical shroud,
Wish upon us, and join the crowd!

Winged Secrets at Eventide

When twilight giggles, creatures play,
With wings that flap in a silly ballet,
A squirrel dons a tiny cap,
As shadows dance, and giggles clap.

The hoot of an owl, a funny sound,
While rabbits hop and spin around,
A nighttime party in the trees,
With winks and nods among the leaves.

Stars join in with sparkling wink,
While crickets play a tune to think,
A mouse brings cheese, in socks it's dressed,
As laughter spreads, all feel blessed.

A nightingale croons a favorite joke,
While shadows mingle, a curious folk,
In this odd gathering under the sky,
The evening's laughter will never die.

Flights Through the Veil

In the dusk where shadows roam,
A duck on a skateboard finds its home,
With feathered friends all in a line,
Zooming through the twilight, feeling fine.

A bat with glasses flies by fast,
Cracking jokes as he zips past,
While fireflies twinkle in the air,
Like tiny lights that just don't care.

A raccoon wearing a bowtie smiles,
He tells a story that spans for miles,
Of fluffy dreams and glittering sights,
In the veil where mischief ignites.

Their laughter echoes as they glide,
Adventures vivid across the tide,
In this flight, they're never shy,
With giggles scattered in the sky.

Shimmering Feathers of Nightfall

As night descends in twinkling spree,
A chicken darts from tree to tree,
With sparkles bouncing, bright and gay,
Playing hide-and-seek till break of day.

A llama in pajamas peeks around,
While crickets sing without a sound,
The stars above, a giggling crowd,
As nighttime whispers feathery loud.

They swap their tales of goofy grace,
With owls who've lost their flying space,
And squirrels that juggle acorns wide,
In this shimmering world, joy can't hide.

The laughter bubbles, a playful tide,
In this night where whimsy won't subside,
As dreams take wing and soar anew,
With funny secrets stitched in dew.

Nocturnal Rhapsody

When the moon smiles, laughter flows,
A hedgehog in a tutu goes,
Waltzing 'neath the starry dome,
Each twirl a giggle in the gloam.

A shy fox with a bowler hat,
Overslept and met the bat,
They swap their hats in friendly jest,
While glowing mushrooms host a fest.

With turtles sporting funky shades,
In this nocturnal masquerade,
The laughter and the mirth prevail,
As silly tunes weave through the veil.

From every nook, songs rise like cream,
In this rhapsody of a silly dream,
Where nighttime's tales are spun with cheer,
And funny antics bring us near.

Silhouette of Mystery

In shadows, whispers softly sway,
A dance of shapes that roam and play.
With giggles lost in moonlit air,
They chase the stars without a care.

A riddle wrapped in silly jest,
A peekaboo where none would rest.
Like poltergeists on painted walls,
Their laughter rings, yet no one calls.

A game of hide and seek they make,
In laughter, secrets gently quake.
For in the night's flamboyant guise,
The mystery wears comical eyes.

The Flight of Hidden Dreams

In slumber's flight, they took to air,
With goofy grins and wild hair.
They soared through clouds of candy floss,
In search of worlds that never cross.

Behind the scenes of sleepy night,
A circus blooms, a comical sight.
Where dreams wear polka dots and stripes,
And giggles echo, dizzy types.

With kites of laughter, spirits roam,
In lands where silliness feels like home.
A symphony of chuckles bright,
In hidden dreams, they take their flight.

Voiceless Flutters

A flutter here, a wiggle there,
Invisible antics fill the air.
With snickers tucked in every nook,
A silent playbook, come take a look!

Whispers of joy, a floating spree,
No voices heard, just glee and spree.
Like butterflies on secret quests,
In the hush of night, they jest and jest.

Behind the scenes, a chuckle stirs,
Where quiet antics make it purr.
Each ripple brings a smile so bright,
In veiled performances of delight.

Darkened Flightpaths

In twilight's hue, they take to flight,
With crooked beams and hearts alight.
They trace their paths in goofy arcs,
Across the sky, igniting sparks.

With shadows long and mischief grand,
They flit and flutter, hand in hand.
Like jesters prancing, wild and free,
In darkened realms, they find their glee.

For every cloud they pirouette,
A nod to silliness, don't forget.
Upon these paths where smiles unfold,
The night is young, the tales are bold.

Plumage Wrapped in Enigma

In shadows, the quirk of a riddle unfurls,
A chicken dances, while the doves twirl.
With a top hat pulled low, and a wink of surprise,
The grand show begins, under moonlit skies.

A parrot recites, with a flair and a squawk,
While owls share their gossip on a late-night walk.
A peacock named Larry, in socks that are bright,
Wanders the stage, oh what a delight!

A duck tries to tango, but slips on the floor,
The crowd erupts, laughter's the core.
With each silly move, the secrets unwind,
In this whimsical world, joy's intertwined.

The spotlight flickers, a bat takes the lead,
With a dance that's absurd, and no sense of speed.
As giggles erupt, in the midst of the jest,
Who knew wingtips could become quite the fest!

Glistening Secrets of the Abyss

Down below the waves, where silliness swims,
The octopus juggles, while the blowfish grins.
Seahorses prance, in a two-step so bold,
Their tales shimmer bright, as the stories unfold.

A crab cracks jokes with a wink and a nudge,
While clams whisper secrets, they never judge.
An eel plays the ukulele in style,
Its tunes make the jellyfish sway for a while.

The mermaids all gather, in glittering glee,
With laughter that echoes from the deep, wild sea.
A whale offers punchlines, huge and profound,
While starfish clap hands, in a rhythm unbound.

In the depths of the ocean, hilarity reigns,
With goggle-eyed fish sharing whimsical gains.
As bubbles ascend, caressing the dark,
The fun's in the abyss, with humor's own spark!

The Magic of Hidden Aviaries

In a nook of the garden, where giggles take flight,
The sparrows conspire, in the silvery light.
With bow ties and berets, they hold a grand ball,
As the fluttering friends span wide, oh so tall.

A robin, quite cheeky, prepares a grand toast,
To the laughter of chicks who are noisy the most.
With a wink and a chirp, they dance in a line,
Creating a scene, both delightful and fine.

A canary's got rhythm, with beat-boxing flair,
While a crow spreads the news, with a theatrical air.
As the crickets join in, with a rhythm so neat,
They turn the whole night into a whimsical feat.

With twirls and with spins, they sing songs of delight,
Whispering secrets through the cool, quiet night.
In this world of pure laughter, oh, what a parade,
In the magic of feathers, new joys are displayed!

Starlit Whispers on the Wind

When the moon sits high, and the stars take a peek,
The fireflies gather, all graceful and sleek.
With winks and soft giggles, they dance 'round a tree,
Creating a spectacle, wild, bright, and free.

A squirrel tells stories of acorns and prizes,
While a hedgehog chuckles at well-hidden surprises.
As rabbits do flips, in a moonbeam's embrace,
The night wraps its arms, in a magical space.

In the breeze, a whisper, a light-hearted tease,
Of antics and pranks that are sure to please.
With twinkling delight, the night feels alive,
With critters and chuckles that leap and then dive.

Once the dawn peeks in, with its warm glowing light,
The secrets of night fade, but the laughter feels right.
In dreams, we'll remember the whimsy and glee,
Of starlit whispers that are wild and carefree!

www.ingramcontent.com/pod-product-compliance
Lightning Source LLC
Chambersburg PA
CBHW060117230426
43661CB00003B/228